CW01511637

# CONNL____ YOUR CIRCLE

## Learn how the Five Elements can help you be a more authentic you

*by*

# LETA HERMAN
# & JAYE McELROY

{ Authors *of*
THE ENERGY OF LOVE }

www.ConnectingYourCircle.com

Connecting Your Circle: Learn How the Five Elements
Can Help You Be a More Authentic You
Copyright © 2014 by Leta Herman and Jaye McElroy
All Rights Reserved

FIRST EDITION
First Printing, January 2014

Copyeditors: Stephen J. Herman, Ph.D. and Jennifer Abbingsole
Cover Designs: Jaye McElroy and Michael Nelson
Interior Design: Jaye McElroy, Leta Herman, and Michael Nelson
Photography: Jaye McElroy

All rights reserved.
No part of this book may be reproduced in any form by any means,
including Internet usage, without the written permission of
Born Perfect® Ink. This includes reprints, excerpts, photocopying,
recording, or any future means of reproducing text.

To reproduce any part of this book, except brief quotations
embodied in critical articles and reviews,
please seek permission first by contacting us at
www.BornPerfectInk.com

Born Perfect® Ink
72 Center St.
Third Floor
Northampton, MA 01060, USA
www.BornPerfectInk.com

Published in the United States of America by Born Perfect® Ink
ISBN: 978-0-9912366-1-9

Who
are
you?

# THREE LITTLE WORDS

Three easy words. Nine little letters. A simple question we want to ask. But this simple question may not be so easy to answer. These three little words we want to ask you are, "**Who are you**?"

Sounds easy right? Well, you'd be surprised at what this question does to people. If someone asks it, you might have a nice packaged answer, like, "I'm a lawyer." Or, "I'm a stay-at-home Mom." Or how about . . . "I am a Red Sox fan!" Perhaps you have prepared a more detailed answer like, "I am a physical therapist who lives in Boston with my partner, and we have a pug named Big Papi."

It's an answer that will likely get most askers off your back. But we're a bit more stubborn than that.

What if we replied with, "No, truly, WHO are you, *really*?" Then what? Awkward pause perhaps?

Over and over again, we have seen this question fluster people so much that they start fumbling for words, have long pauses, or even try to change the subject!

Actually, in all fairness, it can be very hard to express in words who you are *truly*. The ancient Chinese philosophers had a way to explain who you are that goes deeper than your career, your hobbies, or your life situation. They found a way to understand your true nature energetically, called **the Five Elements**. These Five Elements describe energetically who you are at a much deeper level than what you *do* in life. They can even give you the key to what *motivates* you to do the things you do.

We are asking you to open your eyes, your mind, and your heart to learn about the energy of life, the Five Elements, and how they shape and move you energetically every second of your life.

*Connecting Your Circle* is about your energy—your life force, your essence. Your energy is surging through you and unconsciously telegraphs your nature in every word you speak, the look in your eyes, the way you walk, the way you dance, the way you make love . . . basically every move you make exhibits who you really are. Your energy flow never stops and never rests. Even when you're sleeping, it is emanating from your first breath to your last. It is part of you. It is *your* energy signature.

Every living thing on the planet, big or small, has the Five Element energies (Wood, Fire, Earth, Metal, and Water) guiding their every movement. You were born with a particular mix of these Five Element energies that we like to call your Energy stack. They are in a particular order called your **Elemental Energy type**. Your first Element is who you are or truly want to be in your life and dictates a natural but often unconscious tendency to walk, talk, and move a particular way. The order of your remaining Elements influences how you behave in difficult situations.

This book can help you understand your true nature and exactly how your Elements are stacked up in you! *Connecting Your Circle* will give you the words, definitions, the ability to converse about the Five Elements, and the consciousness about who you are so you can be more confident, more aware, and more excited about your life. Once you understand who you are, you can begin to maximize your true potential in ways you've never known before.

This isn't a "self-help" book. It is a "self-acceptance" book. We don't believe you're wrong, broken, or in need of a brain transplant. (Yes, we have had people so frustrated with their lives, they kiddingly ask for the "ole brain transplant." Well, we hope they were kidding!) For the record, we think you're perfect just the way you are . . . you just need to hear that you are perfect, see it, and really feel it in a positive way.

Let's face it. The world is full of people who want you to *change*. They're everywhere . . . businesses want you to buy products to look, feel, and act differently. The media floods us with images, words and thoughts that we are not good enough unless we buy product X, wear product Y, or think Z way—their way of course.

People will hand you a criticism or label every day of your life, whether they are aware of it or not. What you do with those words (or actions) is up to you. Some people cope or deal with such assaults better than others, and no one is immune 100% of the time. In the Mental Health field alone, the descriptions of people and their disorders are growing . . . ADD, AD/HD, OCD, ODD. It's starting to feel like a "Learning Your ABCs" afternoon lesson on Sesame Street! It's no wonder that people (who are trying to be someone they're not) want to pop Adderall with their pancakes for breakfast, Prozac with their pizza for lunch, and Ambien with a side of cookies for a bedtime snack (BONUS: if the drugs don't help you feel better, the sugar, flour, and cheese might numb the pain!).

Millions of people around the world are trying to make themselves perform, conform, and/or forget who they really are. While we mostly want to grow throughout our lives, we don't want that growth to change our true selves. In fact, most people want the opposite. It's what each and every one of us wants deep down inside. We actually want to *be true to who we are*. No matter how you say it. No *exceptions*. (At least not yet!)

"Sit still!" "Get Going!" "Speak up!" "Stop talking so much!" "Don't be so silly!" "Can you be more serious?" "Stop being so serious!" "Be more assertive!" "Don't be intimidating!" "Be nicer!" "Be tougher!" "Don't be a sissy." "Don't be so neat." "Get organized!" "Why are you so stupid?" "Don't be such a know-it-all!" "What is wrong with you?"

These types of comments mold us, form us, make us fit into something or someone we're *not*! As a child, maybe you tried to conform to those around you. Or maybe you rebelled like crazy to be yourself despite what your parents and teachers said. Either way, you may have compromised yourself and developed habits of compensation that made you feel like you're not yourself. Many of us continue to do this everyday without realizing it.

So if your deep desire is to be yourself, then who are you now?

## New learning from ancient wisdom

Lucky for us someone already did the heavy lifting a long time ago and actually figured out how to explain who you truly are.

It's this philosophy that we've been studying for many years now, and we want to share this knowledge through writing this book.

Over two thousand years ago Ancient Chinese philosophers came up with a language, a way to explain a person's true nature.

This philosophy is called the Five Elements.

You have all Five Elements within you. We all do. However, your first Element (sometimes called your primary Element) is the one you really identify with and is your motivation or Elemental style that carries you, energetically throughout your life. You will always be *that* Elemental Energy type your whole life, even if you've tried (or were forced) to be someone you're not or you've somehow learned to develop one of your other Elements more strongly.

At the most basic Elemental level, the ancient Chinese believed you don't really have a choice how your Elements were determined since they were present when you were born. Your motivations in life, your reason for being, and your impetus for being alive are some of the things you can begin to look at from a different perspective once you know the order of how your Elements stack up.

When you learn about your Elemental Energy type, you can begin to maximize the things you're naturally good at and minimize the things you aren't so good at. Getting clarity about the strengths of your primary Element will help you in a multitude of situations and personal communications. But the power of the Five Elements doesn't stop there. Once you learn to manifest your own Elemental energy in your life, you can then learn how to develop the other

Elemental energies in yourself. We call this Connecting Your Circle. This book is about first recognizing and accepting who you truly are, and then, from that place of acceptance, you can further develop all Five Elements in yourself. In other words, you become a true master of your own energy and thus connect your own Five Element circle.

## It's a small world and getting smaller and smaller

Every society has a dominant set of values that people in that society are often expected to follow. Even those who rebel against their society's values are usually still working within them. The culture, Elementally speaking, in the United States is Wood—we are taught from a young age to always strive to be the best we can be at whatever we're good at. This works great for the Woods growing up here in the US, who are rewarded for being the natural born leaders that they are. But what about the Earths, who by nature just want to support everyone else and are not so focused on winning all the time? Theoretically if all Five Elements are equally represented in the world (and there's no way to know if that's true), there are just as many Earths in the United States as Woods, but their strengths don't dominate the cultural viewpoints in the U.S. How can Earths be their authentic selves when they've been raised in a culture that's focused on winning?

In England or Japan—both Metal societies—respect, service, rules, rigor, and obedience are prized. These aspects can make the culture seem emotionally reserved. How do the Fire people—who are emotionally expressive and least likely to follow the rules—make it in those kinds of cultures?

France—an Earth-based society—is a country where culture, thought-provoking conversations, and four-hour, no-rush dinners are often treasured. (Can you see that happening on a wide-scale in the U.S.?) How do the Woods, who move so fast and make split-second decisions, thrive and survive in that kind of culture? Or in Italy or India, both Fire cultures, where lively interactions, humor, extensive entertainment, and love are most valued, where do the quiet Metals go to get away and find peace? Let's consider China, a Water culture, very ambitious but somewhat disorganized and unpredictable. How do the Earths, who love to plan ahead, keep things orderly, and create rhythm in life, find fulfillment there?

There are hundreds of other societies and countries, each cherishing a different set of values and cultural nuances that sometimes fit only a small group of their citizens. To break down society even smaller, there's your state, your city, your neighborhood, your side of the tracks, and then there's your family. Big pause there. Your family is a significant part of how you grow up no matter where you live in the world. The caregivers who raise you will indeed influence your cultural references and traditions.

The questions are: Does your energy match the culture you grew up in or your family's values? Yes or No? What Elemental Energy type are your parents? Did they help or hinder you? Did they raise you to be who you truly are or who they wanted you to be? Perhaps they raised you to be like them—putting a totally different type of energetic pressure on you? Sometimes this can be the square peg in the Elementally round hole . . . not a good way to do it, but darn it, your parents will make that peg fit into that hole no matter what! We all try to fit into many different situations one way or another. Some of us are masters at it. Yet accepting who you are can be very confusing with all the messages you've been getting from society, family, friends, lovers, co-workers, and bosses.

The clear thought here is, if you do not search for your true self, who will? It's time to find a way to get in alignment with yourself. It sounds like a new age tagline, but it is simply the easiest way we can say it. If you don't care, if you don't try . . . well, maybe you need to put this book back on the shelf, or hit the delete from your Kindle now. If that is kinda gloomy, well wait a second . . . the good news is *we care*. Yes, we are giving you the information to try and start the search, head down the path, look in your own mirror to see what you want to see.

The first four chapters of *Connecting Your Circle* will help you get an idea of who you are Elementally and what that means in your life. Once you understand which Elemental Energy type you are and what that means, you can be strong and powerful in who you are at times when those strengths are required. In other words, you can learn to utilize the strengths of your Elemental Energy type and not be so thwarted by its weaknesses.

You can then begin to learn how to access the other Elements within you. You can tap into all Five Elements inside you with amazing results. *Chapter Five* will discuss how you can learn to adapt and adjust effortlessly to another way of doing things without any self-judgment. You can learn to communicate successfully in any type of encounter or relationship.

For example, if you're someone who quietly hangs back, perhaps doesn't like large groups, and yet looks mysterious and kind of cool to other people, you are likely to have the Elemental Energy type of Metal. This is your main Element as you travel through life. However, when you are learning to **Connect Your Circle**, you can move in and out of your other four Elements when needed or desired. When you perhaps need to be assertive and outgoing, you can draw upon undeveloped parts of yourself, such as tapping into your Wood or Fire Elements, which easily engage with others on a social level. These two Elements seem more at ease at social events, family gatherings, or in the business world.

## Celebrity Watching

Celebrities, famous people, and movers and shakers around the world can be easily seen in the public eye. Almost all cultures love to love their celebs. These people are paraded in front of us 24/7, in every medium possible, from television and *People* magazine to the latest of YouTube, Facebook, Instagram, and Twitter instantly capturing, recording, and reporting their movements from place to place, from moment to moment.

The world is getting much smaller in terms of how we can connect with anyone on the planet in a blink of an eye. What an amazing concept! These changes are really making the world a smaller place, smashing boundaries and distances in the second of time it takes to hit the view button on your smart phone.

Watching how people move and talk is one of the best ways to learn about the Five Elements. TV and the Internet have made it easier to find real examples of the Five Elements in motion. Let's examine how various celebrities exhibit the Five Elements for all of us to see and share almost 24 hours a day. Since many of us can access and study our celebrities online in many ways, the Internet has become a powerful teaching tool for Five Element students. We had so much fun with our look at celebrities that we decided to give you a sneak peak of *Chapter Four: Channeling Your Inner Celebrity* right now.

What do Oprah, George Clooney, and Hillary Clinton all have in common? They are all **Wood** Elemental Energy types. If needed, they are very comfortable being at the forefront and taking center stage. They have a commanding presence and are natural born leaders. When they speak, people listen. They stand for things that matter and believe they are working for the betterment of the world. They wear the white hat, not quietly like some people do. No, they're loud like a bullhorn in the world, telling us about what needs to change to make the world a better and fairer place for everyone.

While their personalities differ, their energies and the way they move through the world are very similar indeed. They think fast and keep conversations moving. Motivated to be as great as they can be, they move rapidly through life and stand for what they think is right over and over again. Do you relate to this kind of energy?

How about Julia Roberts, Cate Blanchett, or David Letterman? What do they all have in common? They all are **Fire** Elemental Energy types. Their focus is on people and sharing through conversation and heart connection. When they sit down and chat, their words aren't as important as their presence and their smiles (though they might be passionate about their important topics and get the listeners excited). It's more about their energy, the light banter, the gentle teasing, and the bright eyes that gaze sometimes shyly into the other person's. They have a light sense of humor and connect through a subtle joy in their sharing of stories. They have a vulnerability that allows them to connect with you through their hearts and sweep you away for a moment. They love to laugh and shine brightly for the whole world to see. Do you ever feel this way?

Maybe you're more serious than a Fire person? Perhaps you're a thinker, which is the **Earth** Elemental Energy type. Barack Obama, Jennifer Aniston, and Beyoncé are all strong Earth. They are people-focused like the Fire Element, but more in a community-building way. They are the thinkers (and listeners) and like to gather everyone together to solve problems. They get people on board and build consensus. They are the fixers in the world. Fixing isn't just about resolving the problem but also about the emotional implications of what people are doing and why. They like people to be kind and considerate to one another. They give of themselves and share their knowledge with anyone asking for help. Are you that go-to person in your circle of family and friends?

Perhaps you're quiet, brooding, or mysterious-looking like Angelina Jolie, Johnny Depp, and Marilyn Monroe. This is the **Metal** Elemental Energy type, with its cosmic reflections on life. Metals like to wait and watch the world from a distance. Other people are fascinated by the Metal allure and want to know more about them. Metals don't share themselves unless a person is being completely sincere and open with them. Otherwise they remain aloof and at a distance. When Metals sense a person's sincerity, they really connect and engage in a deeper dialogue. Big parties with tons of fake conversations and false personas–they'd rather stay home, read a book or watch an old movie, and chill. Sound familiar to you?

Could it be you feel more awkward and quirky, in a fun-loving, silly kind of way? Robin Williams, Whoopi Goldberg, or Jack Black are examples of the **Water** Elemental Energy types. The fun for them is in being more crazy and different than the rest of us. Waters rule the world of comedy, so laughing and being funny is a big part of this celeb list. Waters are unpredictable. On the one hand, they can be more like a still pond and sit on the couch chilling (looking like a Metal person), just restoring energy. On the other hand, they might never stop moving, like a rushing river. Both these kinds of Water types are unpredictable and ready to go from zero to 60 miles per hour in a split second if something intense is about to happen. They are always ready for anything. Drama and intensity is what life's about. Are you feeling the Water vibes?

You're much more like your famous Elemental celebs than you think! If you're a Metal, it doesn't matter whether you're a famous celebrity walking the red carpet or a goat herder in the mountains of Nepal, you have the same basic energy qualities. Once you begin to learn about the Five Elements, you will be able to see similarities and differences in yourself and in every person you meet! Fun, fun, fun.

Go with the
flow...

# WHAT IS Qi?
# SAY CHEE-SE PLEASE

To explain this big idea of *qi* (or *chi*, pronounced like "chee"), we're going to have to cover a little science first. We promise it won't be long and boring. There might be a pop quiz at the end (okay, there is a quiz at the end of Chapter 3), but don't panic. You can't fail this quiz. We are going to keep this simple, really easy. People spend their entire lives studying this "stuff," so think of this as a quick primer to all the most important answers of life. Hah! If it were only that simple!

This chapter is a reference chapter for discussions to follow. So at any time you can refer back to it. Let's get started on the story of energy. A long time ago in a galaxy far, far away . . . . Hold on! That's another story.

Thousands of years ago (exactly how long no one really knows, but probably close to 3000 years), ancient Chinese philosophers developed theories about *qi*. Similar to how modern physicists observe nature to develop theories of velocity and relativity, these philosophers examined the synchronicity of life and the delicate balance of living creatures on the planet. They believed the most important thing that every living being on the planet shared was... **ENERGY**. Let's try to understand energy and the lessons that the ancient teachers tried to impart.

## Go with the flow . . .

Energy moves in humans like the electricity delivered to power outlets, say in our houses. You can't actually *see* the electricity. You can't grasp it, although it can electrocute you if you get too close. You can't smell it—well, if you do, it's time to call the Fire Department! But, seriously, you know it's there because it turns on lamps, heats toasters, and makes all our TVs and computers work like magic. But short of sticking your finger in the socket to actually feel electricity's power, we all believe it's there even if we can't see it.

In all living organisms, including you, *qi* is the energy coursing within you. It's your electricity, so to speak. It flows through you and radiates from you. All humans have their own set of internal power lines, and if you put a person's power lines all together, they form a power grid in the body. These power grids, in humans, are called *meridians*.

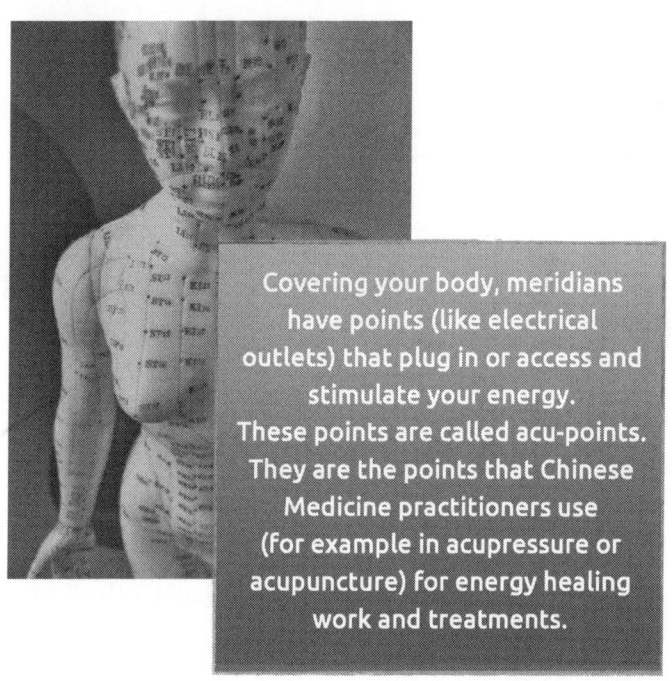

Covering your body, meridians have points (like electrical outlets) that plug in or access and stimulate your energy.
These points are called acu-points. They are the points that Chinese Medicine practitioners use (for example in acupressure or acupuncture) for energy healing work and treatments.

Your *qi* is your power and your life source, animating your body. It's the reason you move the way you move. Ancient Chinese masters created a vocabulary to describe the movement of *qi*. The most basic movements of *qi* are *yin* and *yang*.

The Taijitu yin/yang symbol can be seen throughout the world, from ancient monasteries to the bottom of kids' skateboards. But most people don't know what it actually means or signifies. Do you know? (Wait don't run off to Google it . . . we will tell you!)

The famous *yin/yang* symbol shows you the simplest movement of . . . you guessed it, *the energy in life.*

*Yin* energy descends and condenses.

*Yang* energy ascends and expands.

Think of the geyser Old Faithful going off as *yang.*

After the geyser goes off, all the water is sucked back into a hole in the ground, compressing and building power as *yin*. To see a short video of an actual geyser in Iceland showing both of the *yin* and *yang* states, visit our web site: http://www.ConnectingYourCircle.com/geyser/

Often unknowingly, we compare the *yin* and *yang* energies in our daily life, using different labels to name it. For example, we might say that someone who is outgoing and the life-of-the-party is more *yang* than the quiet wallflower who is more *yin*.

Or maybe we contrast people who don't speak up for themselves (*yin*) vs. those who stand up and fight (*yang*), even on behalf of others who are unable to (*yang*). The energy of *yin* and *yang* shifts constantly and is unpredictable.

*Yin* and *yang* are the building blocks of your new energy vocabulary. However, the Chinese masters believed that life needed a more complex language to describe how human beings move, act, and interact with each other. That's where the Five Elements come into play.

## It's Elemental, my dear Watson!

To understand who you are, let's first understand the energy or *qi* in each Element. How does each Element move differently from the other Elements? We can think of the five forms of energy as a continuum from *yang* to *yin*. Picture them on a circle, starting with Wood (little *yang*) on the left, then Fire (big *yang*) at the topmost *yang* position of the circle, to Earth (balanced *yin* and *yang*) to Metal (little *yin*) and finally to Water (big *yin*) at the bottom, the most *yin* part of the circle.

We can put Earth, often called the Fifth Element, in between the more *yang* Elements (Wood and Fire) and the more *yin* Elements (Metal and Water).

The Five Elements

Wood ———▶ Fire ———▶ Earth ———▶ Metal ———▶ Water

Or we can show Earth in the center of the circle to portray the balance of *yin* and *yang* circling around the most balanced Element, Earth.

The Five Elements are what make people walk, talk, act, and re-act to each other in a certain way.

*Wood* moves out and back, a thrusting motion, a punch in the air. Wood is an example of *yang* energy, like the young sprout bursting through the ground in Spring.

Since you have all Five Elements in you, in a certain order, or stack, you can be like any of them at any time . . . right? Well, yes . . . sort of! Although you could move in different ways Elementally speaking, the ancient Chinese healers believed that you most often move according to your predominant Element.

It's your default behavior, the one you use when you move unconsciously and without inhibitions. You could try to change the way you naturally move, or something might alter your cadence, your posture, or your actual walking stride . . . but we believe your first Element will always be your dominant tendency.

With even more

*yang* energy,

Fire moves up

and down,

likes flames expanding

and wildly dancing.

Let's discuss the order of the Five Elements. As we have said already, we have all Five in each of us in a particular order that gives us our specific energy type or signature. Someone might be Fire/Water/Earth with Metal and Wood last. You might be Wood/Metal/Fire with Earth and the Water Element following. As your level of understanding increases, you'll see how the order of a person's Elemental Energy stack makes a difference.

For most purposes in life, your first Element is what matters most. It is the Element that should ideally occupy most of your time, up to 80 percent. ("Ideally" means you are living a normal life in a supportive environment.) The second Element is also very important. Think of it as enhancing your first Element. Your second Element is more like your backup plan. It's the Element you rely on when your first Element doesn't allow you to fit into a particular social situation. In our opinions, your second Element should be dominant about 15 percent of the time. For example, some Fire people can't help giggling or smiling almost all the time even at a somber event, like a funeral. But laughing at funerals is socially insensitive, so the Fire people have to draw upon their second Element to project a more serious and socially acceptable persona. A Fire person might shift into Metal or Earth energies to be quiet and respectful in this situation.

Your third Element is a place you go to when things go badly for you. It shows up when you're sick, miserable, or depressed. It can help you get back on track when nothing else works. Luckily these hard times are usually few and far between, so we might just spend 5 percent of our time being in our third Element.

Are you wondering how we get our Elemental Energy types and in what order? The first thing almost everyone asks us is: Is it like your horoscope? It is *not* based on your birthdate or birth month. Although the ancient Chinese attribute some astrological influence to your Elemental Energy type, astrology is not the primary root of its origin. Your Elemental Energy type is also not from a magical unicorn that taps its beautiful horn gently on your little baby forehead when you are born. Not from that talking, wizarding, sorting hat straight out of Harry Potter either. Nope. It is actually very easy to explain. The ancient Chinese teachers believed that your Elements are influenced by a combination of your biological parents' energies and the astrological events that are occurring at the time of your birth. So you can't tell people's Elemental Energy type by their birth dates. More likely, their Elemental Energy signature will be inherited from one or both parents, although the imagery of the magical unicorn, we agree, is much more enchanting and certainly more entertaining.

Did you ever feel like an alien visitor from another planet as a child? Did your parents joke that you were switched at birth since you are *so* not like them? Perhaps you heard whispers of a visit from the milkman or maybe from the stork that dropped you off at the wrong house? These sorts of sayings are cruel yet fairly common because some parents just can't imagine their children being so unlike them. Your uniqueness in your family may have caused a few head scratches of confusion as to why you don't think (or act) like everyone else in the household. You could be called your family's Elemental black sheep. But you were probably called a lot of names, so let's not add one more to the pile.

*Earth* moves circularly, reaching out and enveloping you. It is a perfect balance of *yin* and *yang* energies.

Parents and primary caregivers usually like to teach their children to be like *them* (for good or bad). It is what they are and what they know. It's what they think they are supposed to do! This works very well in many cases since children are often like one of their parents. However, if you aren't a little Mini-Me of one of your parents, you might have felt lost or confused about who you are and how you are *supposed* to act. You might have defaulted to your second or third Element and acted like someone else to fit your parents' expectations. In this situation, you're not able to be your authentic self. Most children go through some normal stages of rebellion without trying to change who they fundamentally are. But in this case, the disconnect goes much deeper within a child, which often carries through to adulthood.

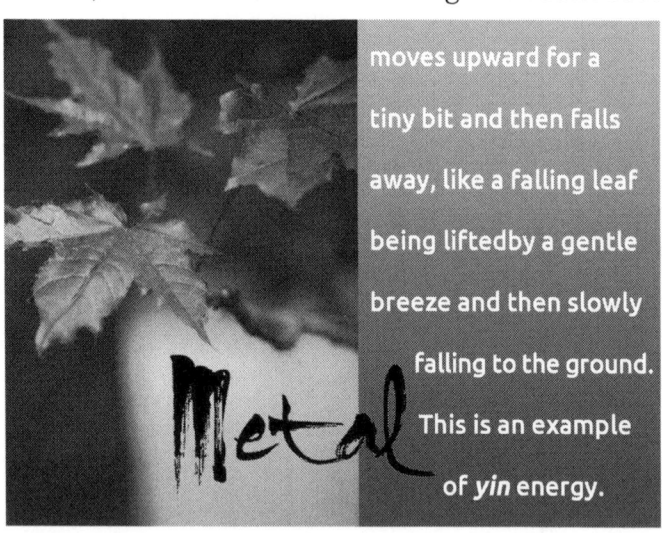

moves upward for a tiny bit and then falls away, like a falling leaf being lifted by a gentle breeze and then slowly falling to the ground. This is an example of *yin* energy.

We've found this condition to be a lot more common than you'd think. It can take years to revert back to your *first* and Elemental self.

If you think this circumstance describes you, it's not so important to figure out your *first* Element right away. You can pick two or three that you identify with most, then think about them for a few days. See what life looks like from each Element's vantage point. Does it feel familiar? Do any resonate? Do you relate to one more than the others? Most people feel like their Element feels like home. But occasionally often due to past trauma, you might not feel comfortable being who you are supposed to be. That's okay. Do your best. This is a gut check time. No B.S. here.

## Love me as I am

Are you wondering if you can change your Elemental Energy type? Change is a beautiful thing in life, but Elementally speaking, the answer is a big, "NO!" Remember, this book isn't about actually changing who you are. In fact quite the opposite. It's about accepting who you are! It is self-awareness, self-acceptance without all the hype.

Still, people ask if they can change their Elemental Energy type because they don't like themselves. We are taught early on in our families or more generally in society to fix mistakes, resolve emotional problems, or fix undesirable situations. We are taught to work on ourselves and change what people think is wrong with us.

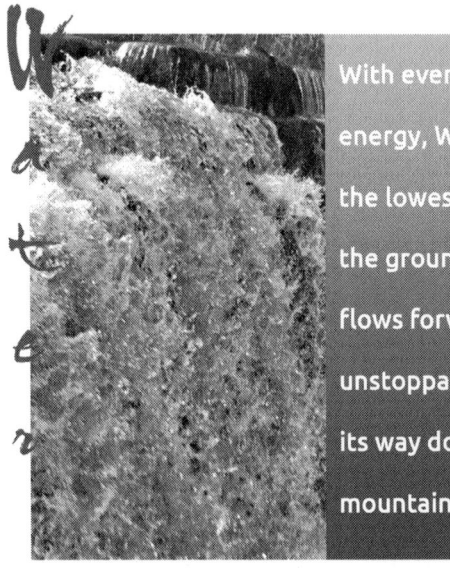

With even more *yin* energy, Water seeks the lowest level on the ground and then flows forward like an unstoppable river making its way down from the mountain to the ocean.

Going back to that big "NO" to changing your Elemental Energy type, we need to acknowledge that not all ancient Chinese masters agreed. Some believed that you could alter your Elemental Energy type through the process of Alchemy, a lifetime of intense self-reflection on your authenticity. In other words, this requires a lifetime of work! But both sides of the controversy agreed that the first step is to *love yourself as you are*. So this book is about that first step, about loving yourself all that you can. Once you love yourself and embrace your Elemental Energy type, in likelihood, you won't want to change. You will want to shout from the rooftops who you are!

# THE SWEET EMBRACE

First, you learn to embrace who you truly are. This will become easier as you identify your Elements. Your Elemental Energy type influences how you love, what kind of career you want to pursue, how you manage money, how you spend your free time, what kind of clothes you like, what kinds of people you want to have relationships with, even what kind of music you like. Yes, each Element has a certain style of music, including rhythms, beats, and lyrics.

## Elemental motivations

When you get down to what really matters most to people, we're not all the same. You'd think we would all have the same motivation or goal in life, such as success, love, family, respect, or fun. But we don't.

Amazingly, we don't all want love or understanding or respect. Your motivation for living ... your *raison d'etre* or reason for being is linked to your Elemental Energy type, which helps us understand what your *true motivation* in life is. It's mind-boggling that after spending five minutes with you, we can know so much about you. When we start to tell people about themselves based on their Elemental Energetic type, suddenly they're nodding and smiling, shocked that we know so much about them in such a short amount of time. This isn't our magical super powers at work... it's as simple as being able to recognize your energy in you.

### What is your Elemental motivation in life?

- If you are **Wood** . . . you want someone to truly see how great you are. You're not fond of making mistakes, and you would rather not dwell on your faults or bad habits. Instead, you prefer to concentrate on all the good reasons that you are successful! Such good news makes you magnanimous. Then you want to reward those around you who are also doing their best.

- If you are *Fire* . . . you want an unconditional love that makes you feel beautiful and adored. You want people to see your beauty despite the blemishes.

No matter how badly you screw up, you want your lover, parents, or co-workers to still love you. You need deep heart connections, those founded on love and sharing similar interests.

- If you are **Earth** ... you like to help people. You also just want to be understood. You want the people in your life to get you on a deep level. If the people in your life understand that all the difficulties you've encountered have made you a better person, they might be able relate to you. You're often searching for friends, family members, lovers, and co-workers, who will say things that validate your emotional states. Understanding has to be expressed in words ... lots (and lots) of words.

- If you are **Metal** . . . you want to be honored and respected. Rather than words, you seek a sense of connection that is more cosmic in nature. It's an acknowledgment that can be shown in a gesture as when a monk bows silently in recognition of services and sacrifices made for others.

- If you are **Water** ... you seek adventure and intensity in life. You connect wordlessly and deeply. Normal surface conversations, which are quite interesting to other Element types, especially Fires, are boring to Waters. Your life is alternating calm and activity. The more you rest, the more energy and intensity you can put out in the thrilling moments. At times you might like living a couch potato's existence, engrossed in TV or video games. Having fun while regenerating your energy is just fine with you.

## Elemental seasons

The Five Elements have always been portrayed in ancient Chinese texts as representative of different seasons of the year. The seasons can help us understand how the Elements explained life as we know it. Even though life appears to begin in Spring, when the first sprouts peek out of the hard ground, we actually begin our story in Winter, which corresponds to the Water Element. *All life begins in Water, in gestation, in the womb of the world.*

### Water

Winter, the time of hibernation, represents the Water Element. As the temperature drops, the movement of Water can come to a near standstill almost freezing and becoming inert. When you are still and quiet, you gather your energy. A huge power builds and condenses, perhaps on top of mountains. The snow and ice lie dormant until Spring when warmer weather melts it back to water, unleashing a torrent of kinetic energy. Another analogy is to think of the pressure that builds deep underground below a geyser. At intermittent times, the geyser erupts when the power builds to a peak. The longer it waits, the greater the pressure, which is why it can be such a huge force in nature. It can go and go and go, like clockwork . . . blow and then rest, blow and then rest, blow and then rest . . . It's relentless. This is the power of Water energy.

Timing is essential. Skill belongs to the Water Element—skill as it relates to flowing just at the right moment and with the right force like an archer taking aim, stretching the bow to its maximum capacity, not a millimeter more, then sucking in and holding the breath, calm and focused, *before* releasing the arrow to fly with full power and accuracy to its target. This analogy represents the peaceful state of plants in the Winter waiting for the moment when Spring arrives.

## Wood

The moment the archer *releases* that arrow, the time of the Wood Element, the season of Spring, has arrived. Now the arrow flies with incredible strength and assertiveness. It's not going to hold back. It was made to fly with precision. It follows the most direct or strategic path and doesn't deviate until the target is reached. This shows the Wood Element's goal-oriented, efficient way of being.

Wood's time is Spring. It's the symbol of the trees that grow in nature when the seeds in the ground surge upwards and break through the barrier of the earth. Wood energy surges forward as directly as possible. If an obstacle, such as a rock, sits in the plant's path, it will find a way to grow around it and continue up. Wood is the Element of action, of doing. Doing is the way of the Wood Element's energy.

As the tiny sprouts burst forth through the ground, they continue their rapid growth. But they also need to put forth leaves and branches in order to survive. So they surge upward for a bit, and then pause, pull back into themselves and shoot their leaves outwards. Then again they move up and then out, advancing and then resting. This is the nature of Wood. Energy flows out and back. For every advance forward in your life, there's a pause to regroup, to gather more energy, to strategize what the next move should be, and then move out again. Like the arrow locked onto its target, Wood energy never loses sight of its goal, even as its energy moves inevitably toward Summer (Fire time).

## Fire

The moment plants reach their full height, they have arrived. In Summer, the season of Fire, the plants reach maturity. They stop their upward surge toward the sky and transition into beautiful blooms. Fire is the Element of beauty and vulnerability. Fire energy slows down and spreads out like a glorious rose in full bloom, beautiful and exuberant, exhibiting itself to the world. Roses say to the world, "Stop and look at me. Smell me. Appreciate my beauty." The saying, "Stop and smell the roses" implies that life is going too fast. Where are you going if you've already arrived? It's time to look around and enjoy Fire's beauty. There are so many glorious varieties of roses to be admired.

The season of Summer represents exposing your vulnerabilities despite potential threats. As an example, consider the vulnerability of the rose's flower. It's not like its stem, so strong and full of thorns. If you brush against the flower, its petals fall off easily. A strong summer storm can overwhelm the rose, scattering its petals to the wind. But after the sun returns, if the rose has life left, it will revive. The actual rose plant can be quite hardy, like a Fire's heart—willing to love again after each heartbreak. Summer glory burns brightly until it begins to wane into the Harvest season—the transition between Summer and Autumn (Earth's time).

## Earth

The day we pick the ripe fruit, the day we reap the harvest of all that maturity, then we have entered Earth's glorious season. Earth is the mysterious Fifth Element. It represents the two-week periods of transition between each of the seasons. Of the four transitions between seasons (Winter to Spring, Spring to Summer, Summer to Fall, and Fall to Winter), it's the bountiful Harvest season time (between Summer and Autumn) that best symbolizes the Earth Element. Earth is about the fullness and ripeness of life. All the storehouses and granaries are full to the brim . . . they are overflowing with the harvest so that everyone can share abundantly with loved ones. Earth loves to celebrate this time of the year. It is your feast, your banquet of the harvest that symbolizes Earth. When you can give away the fruits of your labor, enjoy it among all your friends and family, this is Earth in all its glory.

Earth people know that you can't expect a good harvest without hard-work, dedication, and caring throughout the whole year. The process of giving and receiving requires awareness, thought, and a sense of responsibility. The Earth Element excels at problem solving. For Earths, the greatest gifts you can give are the pearls of wisdom gained from your thoughtful experiences of resolving issues. The sharing of the knowledge gained from your experiences is fundamental to your happiness.

Anyone who is very generous knows that the secret to generosity is being willing to receive. For in order to have something to give, you must receive first. Plants exemplify this principle. They take in the rain and the sunshine all Spring and Summer long before they are able to yield their bounty. Then in Autumn (Metal time), the plants begin the process of decay and return to the earth.

## Metal

At some point after the harvest and the celebration of all that is good and abundant, a moment comes when we must plan ahead for the long, cold Winter. To truly treasure the abundance, we don't want to squander it all at once. Now we've transitioned fully into Autumn, which is all about preparation for a long

Winter's rest. If you have ever made preserves at the end of Summer, you can imagine how those little jars in the basement seem as valuable as gold. Perhaps it's wise not to give *everything* away, says Metal! Let's save some of the bounty for the long Winter. The Metal Element represents people who respect, treasure, and conserve precious items, like rare metals, gems, or jars of jam.

Let's calm ourselves down from the frenzy of summer's exuberance and the sharing of our bountiful harvest. Oh my! This is a time in the seasons of falling back to earth, when all the plants go dormant or die, which brings the cycle back to the essence of things, like when you see the trees without leaves... just the trunk and bare branches. Even the things you're most attached to must leave in the end.

In some traditions the Metal Element is sometimes called the Air Element (also associated with Autumn) because Metal people are like a leaf falling through the Autumn air. The leaf will never be attached to its mother tree again. It must fly free and embrace the free-fall of letting go. What will the letting go bring? It may bring melancholy or longing for the past, and Metal accepts this. But it will also bring new life again in the Spring. As long as you don't cling too tightly or too long, you can relax into the ebb and flow of death and rebirth. And in that silent letting go, that leaf-jumping-off-the-tree moment, you experience the pure exhilaration of the free-fall, which isn't scary at all. Metal people need to trust that the wind will come along and give you an amazing lifetime of magical rides. You fall into life once again like the leaf in the gentle breeze and let life take you wherever it goes.

## Water – Completing the circle

Finally, the moment when the leaf lands on the ground, we have returned to the Water Element and come full cycle in this seasonal journey. The leaf sinks back into the earth, mulches, and integrates into new life. As Winter undergoes its transformation into cold and dark, it amasses the nutrients of the leaf into new energy, so that when Spring arrives, it will be a great new powerful force for rebirth in the world.

Water also waits with anticipation for the right moment to move after being frozen. It's not a passive, sleeping hibernation. It's a waiting watchful guard, for at any moment, one must reach out and grab Spring like catching a shooting star. Springtime is tricky business. Sometimes it has false starts. A warm week followed by a cold snap can be devastating. If a plant springs forth too soon, it could die a premature death. Within a Water person lies a deep knowing. You must choose the right moment to make your move. It's not the kind of knowing that can be studied in school. It's just, well, instinct.

## Your three-legged stool

We have all Five Elements within us in a particular order, which we call your "**stack**." Let's say for example your stack of Elements is Fire/Earth/Water/Wood/Metal. What's most important is to understand what your first three Elements are, what we sometimes call, your "***three-legged stool***." These Elements are the cornerstones of your core authentic self. So in this case your three-legged stool is made up of Fire, Earth, and Water. The remaining two Elements, Wood and Metal, are less important in your life. You're just not interested in those energies most days, so you don't tend to utilize them much. You might care less about the life issues that Wood or Metal people think about, such as being the best you can be or making that cosmic connection. The exception might be when you're bored with your life. In that case, you might feel attracted to someone who is a totally different energy, such as the Woods or Metals. But other than that, you don't feel the need to visit those energies much. Where it's at for you Elementally speaking is your three-legged stool . . . Fire/Earth/Water.

## Walking the walk, talking the talk

The best way to figure out someone else's Element is to watch them in action. The way they walk, the sound of their voice, the way their eyes look at you. This can turn the art of people watching into a whole new sport! But how can you evaluate your own movements through life? With technology today, it is easier than ever to get yourself recorded on smart phones or small video cameras. But even if you watch yourself walk on video, it can be difficult to figure out your own Element all by yourself. You might need a little help from your friends!

Many Five Element enthusiasts have tried to develop on-line or written tests that try to tell you which Element you are. In our experience, many people have taken these on-line tests yet come up with the wrong Element. That's because written tests can only evaluate your personality, not your energy. Your Elemental Energy type explains *how* you move as you do, not what you think. That said, we believe that written tests can help you narrow down your possibilities and will often help you identify which are the first three in your Elemental Stack, just not necessarily in the right order. If you are Fire, Earth and Water, then you'll score highest on those three Elements on a good written test.

## Seconds Please

Figuring out your primary Element is essential so you can start focusing on what's most important in your life or affirm that you are on the right path. But what about your second Element? Your second Element is the energy that can help get you out of social messes and sometimes helps you connect with people who energetically are just not like you at all. It's also important to know if your second Element is the opposite of your first. If so, you might end up beating yourself up a lot or being your own worst critic. Maybe you have a fast Element, such as Wood, as your first and a slow Element, such as Earth, as your second. Challenging? Yes. How would you get anything done? One Element (Earth) is constantly trying to hold back the other (Wood). *People who have an opposing second Element are often very hard on themselves in many ways.* Your second Element can end up shutting down your first over and over again until you learn how to accept who you truly are and lighten up on yourself. When you discover your Elemental Energy type, you can, perhaps for the first time, begin to appreciate your strengths and be a little nicer to yourself.

You'll also want to get to know your third Element, the one you typically go to when you're really miserable (injured, sick, or depressed). When you're in your third Element, because you feel mentally, emotionally, or physically ill, you'll often voice the worst of that Element, as if you've turned everything good about the Element into its opposite. Here is a humorous take on how a person who is sick or down and out might express these third Element gems in challenging times:

- A person with **Wood** third might say with blame–
  "Who the hell got me sick?"
- A person with *Fire* third might cry out–
  "No one really loves me."
- A person with **Earth** third might whine–
  "I can't do this all by myself anymore."
- A person with **Metal** third might drone–
  "I'm never good enough."
- A person with **Water** third might exclaim dramatically–"I just need to lie down before I collapse

from this _____" (insert any injury or sick-
ness, including a simple hangnail).

Maybe these examples will help you keep your
sense of humor the next time you're sick in bed. If
you know what your third Element is, you're more
likely to be able to heal your worst insecurities in life.
Remember, laughter is the best medicine.

## POP QUIZ TIME

So with the goal of discovering your Elements, we've designed something that might help you energetically zone in on your top three. As you read a description of each Element, ask yourself whether you feel the narration describes you or some important part of you. You'll probably know right away which Elements don't! Those you can cross off your list. They are your #4 and #5 Elements. You might relate to your second or third Elements, but it's unlikely you'll have an affinity to your fourth or fifth.

As you take the following *So You Think You Are Elemental Energy* pop quiz, give yourself one point for each statement that you relate to. If you're not sure, guess for now . . .

## Wood

| Do you... | Enter one point for each that describes you. |
|---|---|
| Have an answer for everything? | 1 |
| Act quickly and then reflect on how it went afterwards? | |
| Outwit others very easily? | |
| Always have to have the last word? | 1 |
| Think everyone else is moving in slow motion? | 1 |
| Detest waiting, especially in lines? | |
| Get easily frustrated with society's shortcomings? | 1 |
| Feel tough on the outside but mushy on the inside? | |
| Defend the rights of poor, helpless creatures? | 1 |
| Get easily bored by most people? | 1 |
| Struggled reading this far in the book, not to mention to the end of this list (bonus point!)? | 1 |
| **Total Wood Points** | 2 |

# Fire

| Do you... | Enter one point for each that describes you. |
|---|---|
| Find it nearly impossible to pass a mirror without admiring yourself in it? | |
| Look to see who you know in a room before you notice anything else? | |
| Inject every conversation with your personal life's tidbits? | |
| Laugh inappropriately? | |
| Laugh at almost everything? | |
| Enjoy talking about yourself (See #3)? | |
| Drop everything in your life when a new love interest, hobby, or project appears on the horizon? | |
| Live for love, love to live? | |
| Want everyone to feel the same way about the things you care about? | |
| Express ideas and thoughts in passionate emotional language? | |
| **Total Fire Points** | 3 |

## Earth

| *Do you...* | Enter one point for each that describes you. |
|---|---|
| Like to show people how to do everything? | \ |
| Love when someone asks you for help, advice, or a better way to do a project? | |
| Love sitting in a circle and sharing emotional stories? | |
| Love to host parties with lots of food and good cheer? | |
| Take your time doing important, complex assignments, but can clean your house in no time flat? | \ |
| Think about all the options and analyze all the possible outcomes before making a decision? | \ |
| Like being nice to everyone you know but your family often gets your more witchy side when all their chores aren't done? | \ |
| Wish everyone would respect everyone else's boundaries? | \ |
| Put a lot of thought into giving gifts that really shows people you understand them? | |
| Wish that everyone would appreciate all the thought and effort you put into everything? | \ |
| **Total Earth Points** | 6 |

# Metal

| Do you... | Enter one point for each that describes you. |
|---|---|
| Like to sit back and watch the world go by? | |
| Feel responsible and beholden to many people in your life? | \ |
| Always try to do the honorable thing? | ( |
| Enjoy being of service to others? | ( |
| Want the respect of your friends, coworkers, and family that you rightly deserve? | ( |
| Often look cool and mysterious to others even though you may not see it or feel it? | |
| Avoid large crowds and big parties at all costs (except your favorite music concerts)? | \ |
| Want to hold and touch animals, especially those with fur? | ( |
| Deeply experience things with your five senses, especially smell, taste, and touch? | |
| See things in black and white? | ( |
| **Total Metal Points** | 7 |

## Water

| Do you... | Enter one point for each that describes you. |
|---|---|
| Love friends that make you laugh hysterically? | |
| Seek out intense experiences in life that give you an adrenaline rush? | |
| Like people who don't mind if you're silly, even in public? | |
| Find normal conversation sometimes awkward? | / |
| Think that normal is when a room or car gets cleaned once a year? | / |
| Like to relax on the couch after an exciting event, even for the whole weekend? | |
| Need to move your leg or tap your hand when you're told to sit still? | / |
| Choose to march to your own fashion drummer? | |
| Dislike talking about upsetting events from the past? | |
| Live in the now moment? | |
| **Total Water Points** | 3 |

Which three Elements did you score highest in? So the winner is . . . you! Seriously, your winning three Elements are likely to be your three-legged stool.

You may know instantly what your primary Element is, which is great! Becoming clear about your Elemental Energy type gives you the opportunity to reevaluate your life and how you can live it more authentically. However, if determining your first Element seems elusive, don't be dismayed. It's very common, especially if you are new to the Five Elements. Every person is unique. Not everyone will fit the bill of their Element exactly, but most everyone resonates with a very large percentage of their Elemental traits. There will always be a few exceptions. It can even take years in some rare cases to settle this question, depending on your life situation.

This *So You Think You Are Elemental Energy* pop quiz is meant to give you a general idea of your top three Elements to go along with what you already read in *Connecting Your Circle*. If you scored one Element much higher than the rest, it's likely your primary Element. If you have two or three Elements with high scores, you'll have to read on to gain more insight into the order of your Elemental stack. In addition, each Element is described in much greater detail in the *So You Think You Are . . .* series.

ELEMENTAL ROCK STARS

# CHANNELING YOUR INNER CELEBRITY

$A$ great way to learn about the Five Elements is to observe people. All kinds of people. Yes, people-watching can be more than an amusement or hobby. It can be fun and serve a purpose! Studying people as they walk, talk, and behave in public gives us a way to identify key distinguishing features of each Element. We're not encouraging you to become a stalker or anything annoying or intrusive to anyone else, but rather to become a better student of the Five Elements through keen observation. One of the most fun ways to work these skills is to look at prominent people—such as our celebrities and famous people in the public limelight. After you identify the characteristics of specific Elements and match them to the celebrities, you can compare notes with other Five

Element enthusiasts to see if you are in agreement. In this way you can develop a shared vocabulary of reference points for each of the Elements.

So let's have some fun sharpening our Elemental-detecting skills by looking at some of the movers and shakers of our world today!

## Wood—Who puts the Wood in Holly-Wood?

Wood is big energy in the world, big energy in everyday life, and big energy out in the public's eye. Hollywood is no exception. Famous Wood people are rocking it no matter where they go throughout the world! They are natural born leaders and love to help others reach their goals and dreams. It's no wonder Wood is big and bold, and, for the most part, in love with the public's enthusiasm for their causes. To accomplish their projects, Wood celebrities draw upon their natural gifts of being confident and outgoing.

The Wood Element is assertive and able to converse with just about anyone easily and with good humor. They can talk shop with other actors, rub elbows with the rich and famous, and still be able to have a cup of joe with the local guy on the street—all with ease and sincerity. The wittiest of the Elements, Woods are unusually fast thinkers and very charismatic, able to really turn on the charm, especially when they need it. At the same time they value and can be extremely protective of their personal lives, guarding their privacy zealously. They are the self-declared protectors of all the loved ones in their circle of family and friends, always keeping tabs on everyone's whereabouts (and safety). Although Wood can be bold out in the world, they have another softer side within. They do not always see themselves as the bold trailblazers that they are, so they need lots of people to recognize their "greatness."

## How would you spot a Wood

When looking for Wood celebrities, notice how they walk confidently with their chests forward and elbows coming out at the sides. You can also observe Wood characteristics described in the table on page sixty-four.

Here are some examples of Wood celebrities who embody big Wood energy:

- **Oprah Winfrey**—Oprah's Wood energy helps her think and act quickly, moving her interviews along, saving both her viewers—and, we might add, herself—from boredom. Woods have an amazing ability to think faster and more creatively than any other Element, and Oprah is always one step ahead of her interviewees. Woods also have a way of making whatever they're talking about seem crucial. They want people to learn from whatever the topic is.

## 10 Qualities Wood Would Have

### Look for...

1. **CONFIDENCE**–An assertive and confident nature, especially in the way they hold their bodies and speak.

2. **PRESENCE**–A commanding voice and bossy attitude.

3. **HUMOR**–A flair for witty banter–sometimes fast and furious.

4. **QUICKNESS**–An aptitude for fast thinking with the ability to converse about numerous topics easily.

5. **FOCUS**–Attention to important information.

6. **SOCIAL CONSCIENCE**–A desire for equal fairness and justice.

7. **PERSONAL AIM**–An aspiration to be the best they can be, tackling many different types of projects and hobbies.

8. **CHEERLEADER**–A motivational force for others to do their best and succeed, creating a win/win for everyone.

9. **CONVERSATIONALIST**–A natural ease at engaging people in conversation.

10. **DARING**–An unwillingness to back down in the face of challenges, even unconsciously or consciously seeking them out.

Oprah had the knack of introducing her talk shows in a way that made her viewers want to know what she knows. Oprah also has the Wood ability to retain information and knowledge, making them aware and insightful. Her light humor and banter helps her interviewees feel at ease. She has the boldness and quick wit of Wood, making her truly one of the most influential and powerful social compasses in the world today. Since Wood's goal in life is to be the best you can be, one of Oprah's greatest accomplishments is the empowerment of the women of the world. Way to go, O! We celebrate you daily.

- **Brad Pitt**—Brad is the quintessential Wood guy. Wood people often exhibit ease in the way they walk through and interact with the world. Brad is comfortable within himself. He's very quick to respond to questions about the projects he's promoting with light and witty, off-the-cuff remarks. This attribute is common among many Woods. When speaking to others, Woods also like to engage people, making them each feel like the only person on the planet at that moment in time.

    Brad's completely engaged with whomever he's talking to (often leaning in closer to show his interest). A role model of Wood fairness and honesty worthy of admiration and affection, Brad not only has it all but is doing the right thing and making a difference.

- **Tina Fey**–Tina's book *Bossypants* chronicles this Wood woman's younger years with incredible clarity and honesty. The majority of bosses in the world are Wood because they naturally love to lead and to delegate tasks to others. So her book title is humorous but accurate. Woods really can be, um, bossy! Woods often take on difficult challenges. The more difficult the task, the greater the success! Tina frequently speaks of obstacles in her younger years that she overcame, keeping her moving forward on her path, no matter the hindrances she faced. Very Wood-like of her indeed!

  Woods excel at quick, smart jokes and love to banter with anyone who can keep up with them. Tina's show, *30 Rock*, was one of the fastest moving comedy sitcoms ever on TV. In order to get all the jokes, innuendos, and pop culture references, viewers needed to be completely engaged and on their toes (or watch it twice).

  You'll notice that Wood people often wear

many different hats, not hesitating to step up to any challenge or project that excites them or catches their interest. Tina is a Wood on a mission, tackling and succeeding with numerous ventures at once in the entertainment world. We can't wait to see what's next for this funny powerhouse.

Other great Wood people that we love to watch . . . George Clooney, Tom Cruise, Lady Gaga, Donald Trump, Madonna, Ellen DeGeneres, Pink, Hillary Clinton, Ryan Gosling, Kathy Griffin, Bradley Cooper, Robert De Niro, Will Ferrell, Jennifer Lopez, and Amy Poehler.

These are all powerful and amazing people with their big Wood energy making things happen in the world.

## Fire—Elemental social butterflies

Fire people solicit admirers easily. They smile all the time, and these smiles usually help people feel at ease. Even in day-to-day life, many Fires have a multitude of friends, who may not be truly "close" friends but who often like to *think* they are. Famous Fires are no exception. They are friendly and easy to get along with, and they love social events. They can be the life of the party or sometimes several parties in one night! The Elemental social butterflies, they love to be the center of attention in social settings. Everyone loves Fires because they are so open-hearted. But their open-heartedness comes with a price. When people are mean to them, Fires really take it to heart, making them feel more vulnerable around people they don't know well. Most people don't realize just how vulnerable Fire people really are.

Fires want everyone to like them. In the celebrity world, being as beautiful as possible is often the best way to be liked. Fires struggle if they *think* they have any physical flaws. They know they have so much love and light to give the world, but they often worry that their inner beauty will go unnoticed if people don't see their physical attractiveness. Many Fire celebrities are able to emphasize their beauty and minimize their flaws because the world praises and rewards them well, but chances are, at some point in their lives, they have suffered the bite of meanness. Overcoming heartbreak is one of Fire's points of strength.

Fires love to shine and have as many people see them shining as possible. The more admirers, the more they believe they are beautiful, and the more they can feel safe and overcome their shyness (which is actually fear of being disliked or hurt). This sense of safety helps them put themselves out to the world. But not all Fires are focused exclusively on their beauty. Some pursue knowledge as a way of being admired by their peers, such as becoming a teacher in their field. But the goal is still the same. They want people to like them.

## How to Spot a Fire

When looking for Fire celebrities, notice how their shoulders move (bounce) up and down when they walk. You can also observe Fire characteristics described in the table on page seventy.

Some examples of Fire people shining bright in the world are:

- **Julia Roberts**—If one of the keys to recognizing who is Fire is their smiles and laughter, then Julia Roberts takes the big prize! Every photo, interview, or candid video of her emphasizes her stunning smile. Her laughter is infectious, and she laughs at things even when they may not be exactly that funny or appropriate to everyone else.

  Fire people just can't help looking happy, and Julia is no exception! Remember Fire also is about connection, and Julia excels at making people feel

## 10 Qualities Found in Fire

| *Look for...* |
|---|
| 1. **FRIENDLINESS**–An ever-present smile. |
| 2. **LAUGHTER**–A voice that sounds like it might tip over into laughter at any moment. |
| 3. **OPEN-HEARTED**–Aa ability to make a connection (often asking personal questions about the other person). |
| 4. **ATTRACTIVE**–An attentiveness to personal looks, often unconsciously patting and arranging hair or clothes in public to make sure everything is in place. |
| 5. **PERSONAL SHARING**–A desire to share personal stories when the other person exhibits genuine interest (or not!). |
| 6. **WARMTH**–Warmth that permeates out of them and makes everyone want to smile and fall in love with them–platonically and/or romantically speaking. |
| 7. **VULNERABLE**–Shy when not feeling safe in an environment. |
| 8. **CONVINCING**–An infectious enthusiasm that evokes excitement in others. A great spokesperson for a good cause. |
| 9. **KNOWLEDGEABLE**–An eagerness to share facts they have learned about topics they are interested in. |
| 10. **PEOPLE PLEASER**–A desire to make everyone around them happy, sometimes to a fault. |

special and unique, exuding kindness. However, if you watch her closely, she exhibits that shy, Fire vulnerability as she shifts and moves about uncomfortably. Fires will often unconsciously touch their hair and fidget in their seats, and like

Julia, they will often checks themselves out to make sure they look okay.

Fires often put their power of persuasion to good use and Julia is no exception. She has numerous projects and charities that she contributes to as spokesperson and volunteer around the world. A true Fire woman in every sense—she is kind, loving, and surely the life of the party wherever she goes!

- **Bill Clinton**—Love him or hate him, you have to admit he's one of the most charismatic world leaders of recent history. No doubt, he could charm the pants off anyone (pun intended). We've often said as a joke that Fires could convince you to buy the Brooklyn bridge with their charm. Bill's Fire Element helps him converse and connect easily whether it is with the average guy on the street or a high-level world leader. His success was due to Fire's ability to make a heart connection with people and make them feel special and truly unique in all the world.

  His second secret weapon was Hillary Rodham Clinton, his strong Wood wife, who undoubtedly pushed him in directions that made him stronger. Today, Bill's various philanthropic foundations were founded in conjunction with his wife Hillary and daughter Chelsea. They promote health, economic empowerment, leadership development, and the resolution of racial, ethnic, and religious issues globally. This may be his greatest legacy.

- **Cate Blanchett**—This Academy Award winning actress has played many Wood or Metal characters on the big screen, but when she speaks in her personal life, she is sweet, smiley, and very intelligent with a little bit of shyness, all the main characteristics of Fire.

    If you really take a closer look at all her major roles playing very strong characters, this sliver of Fire vulnerability peaks out in each one. Her ability to be vulnerable even while playing a tough Wood or Metal character is what endears her to her fans. We are glad (dare we say, Galadriel?) to see her keep wearing her heart on her sleeve.

Other Fire people we love to love . . . Anderson Cooper, Lily Tomlin, Bette Midler, Barbara Streisand, David Letterman, Elton John, Ann Hathaway, Amy Adams, Leonardo DiCaprio, Julianne Moore, Drew Barrymore, Sally Field, and pop star Justin Bieber.

These are just a few of the Fire celebrities making us fall in love with them on a daily basis.

## Earth—The fifth Element

The majority of Earths will most likely tell you they prefer to stay behind the stage curtains rather than be front and center. You might find that many of them who work in the entertainment industry actually work backstage, possibly in key production and managerial positions–ensuring that the show does indeed go on.

Although standing in the spotlight isn't easy for them, they can, under special circumstances, be convinced to step out and shine. And when the Earths step out, the world pays attention. They are like the boy or girl next door . . . the world adores them, even despite their faults. Earth Elements are the most patient listeners in the Elemental world. They often are considered by their circle of family and friends to be the "problem solvers." They take this title seriously and truly are the Elemental friends who will listen and listen and listen.

### How to Spot an Earth

When looking for Earth celebrities, notice how their hips move side to side when they walk. You can also observe the Earth characteristics in the table on the opposite page.

Some examples of famous Earths in the world today:

- **Barack Obama**—Barack not only broke the racial barrier to become the first African-American President of the United States, but he also became the first Earth U.S. president in many generations (maybe ever). Since the Earth Element is all about problem-solving, it makes sense that the United States elected him in challenging economic and political times on a global scale. Earth is best at solving problems through consensus-building. Barack brings together teams, including the best thinkers and brightest people he can find to tackle political problems, environmental threats, and economic disasters. We suspect that the main reason that relatively few Earths inhabit the top levels of government and business is they don't tend to go after opportunities as aggressively as the Water and Wood Elements do.

  So how did this down-to-Earth (so to speak) guy get to be the most powerful man on the planet? Well, not to take anything away from Barack since he is truly a hard worker, but he has another secret weapon in his arsenal of talents. Powerhouse

# 10 Qualities Evident in Earth

| *Look for...* |
|---|
| 1. **CONGENIALITY**–Soft eyes, a relaxed smile, and a welcoming face. |
| 2. **CALMING**–A soothing, melodious voice that puts others at ease. |
| 3. **SOCIABILITY**–Friendly and social, happy to be sharing something about themselves. |
| 4. **LISTENER**–An attentiveness that requires taking turns talking (not talking over someone else). |
| 5. **FIXER**–A knack for planning with advanced problem-solving capabilities. |
| 6. **THINKER**–A focus on ideas, philosophies, and analysis of details. |
| 7. **TEAM-PLAYER**–A desire to join groups and help with community projects. |
| 8. **FAMILY-ORIENTED**–An affinity for being part of a family or social group, attending many family events. |
| 9. **NURTURER**–A considerate and caring focus on loved ones and friends (though sometimes they end up being bossy with those closest to them). |
| 10. **APPRECIATION**–A grateful nature that recognizes when others are helpful. Wants others to truly *understand* them and not think they are too demanding. |

Wood wife Michelle stands beside him. She brings the intelligence and strategic thinking of a Wood nature to their partnership. She is the wind uplifting his sails, providing the strong gust he needed to propel him through the rough and tumble world of politics and into the White House. An Earth/ Wood team is a force to be reckoned with and gets a lot accomplished in the world! Wood holds the vision and sets the course while Earth contributes the planning skills and hard work and to get there.

- **_Jennifer Aniston_**—She is truly the Earth girl next door . . . sweet, kind, and caring, yet alive and strong-minded in her own way. Earths are often very balanced in their nature, and Jennifer is a great example of how Earth can be a mix of sweetness and extroversion at the same time. Her on-screen roles often portray more ordinary women who are making their way through the world with their own style. Neither too flashy nor pretentious, she's the perfect Earth woman to share solid ground and the stage with. She's also smart and uses her brilliantly balanced Earth mind to think problems through in order to find the best solution for everyone.

  Earth people always consider everyone who will be affected by a decision before moving forward. No doubt she is the big listener and problem solver in her circle of "Friends"—we couldn't resist one Rachel comment!

- **Beyoncé Knowles**—Here is one Earth girl who is on top of the world right now! However, she does it in typical Earth fashion, including having many other performers surrounding her to share the stage. If you ever see a Beyoncé performance, it is a community event for sure. Beyoncé may be the big star, but everyone around her is important to her overall vision of her work. She's very rarely alone on stage, and if she is, it's not for long before a bevy of dancers join her. It truly takes a village to put on a Beyoncé show.

  Earths also want to be understood. When on stage, Beyoncé likes to make sure that everyone is listening to her and that we all "get her." Being understood was the goal of her 2013 documentary special *Beyoncé : Life Is But a Dream*, which revealed her deepest feelings and motivations in Beyoncé style.

  Like many other successful Earth people, Beyoncé didn't start alone. She began her early career in the singing group Destiny's Child where all members shared the limelight and the rewards equally. Her Wood father was the impetus that helped Beyoncé move into a solo career. But it is her commitment to hard work that has made her one of the most influential powerhouse Earths to watch in the world today. Believe us when we say, Beyoncé, we're *listening*, and we really *do* get you!

Some examples of other Earths stepping out into the spotlight:

U2's Bono, Lisa Kudrow, Christina Aguilera, Michael Franti, Kristin Wiig, Kerry Washington, Javier Bardem, and Zachary Quinto.

These are strong, dependable people who are bringing Earth energy to the world.

## Metal—The cutting edge

The alluring mystery of Metal makes for some of the biggest movie stars in history. They are quiet in general but can become talkative when you finally get them interested. Most of the time, they happily hang back and watch the world go by. When Metals walk, they seem to almost float on air, adding even more to their incredible sex appeal. Even when they do smile, they often appear far away, just out of the grasp of many. They make audiences want more, want to possess them, and want to hang out and party with them, but they never can. It's impossible to possess a phantom that always just floats away out of reach.

## How to Spot a Metal

When looking for Metal celebrities, you can notice how their heads are held high but their arms look floppy when they walk. You can also observe the Metal characteristics described in the table on the next page.

Here are a few Metals who are bright and shining like polished Metal:

- **Angelina Jolie**–The quintessential Metal Element person. She has the sultry walk, the sexy voice, and the coolness factor that is so Metal. Angelina is intelligent, kind, fair, and loves to be both sensual and alluring on screen and off. Her Metal reverence is apparent in her acting style as well as in real life. Although she sometimes plays strong Water (and Metal-ish) characters (Lara Croft, Evelyn Salt), she manifests a mysterious quality, a certain aloofness, that makes people want to know more about her.

    She is a perfect example of how Metal seems to be little engaged in the world yet everyone around them pursues them to find out what they think. To study the near perfect Metal walk, watch Angelina–complete with arms dangling and head

# 10 Qualities Materializing in Metal

| *Look for...* |
|---|
| 1. **Aloofness**–A tendency to stand on the edge of a crowd, watching and waiting. |
| 2. **Coolness**–An ability to be someone that others want to emulate. A coolness factor that is hard to describe, but you know it when you see it. |
| 3. **Sex appeal**–An alluring and mysterious quality, with a slow, sultry walk. |
| 4. **Regalness**–Head held high, almost appearing snooty or superior looking. |
| 5. **Reserved**–A quiet voice that forces people to really pay attention to hear them. |
| 6. **Hard**–A surprising toughness that comes out when pushed (can play very tough characters in movies). |
| 7. **Admired**–A person who commands respect from everyone. |
| 8. **Malleable**–An ability to transform into many types of characters effortlessly. |
| 9. **Private**–A tendency to enjoy being quietly acknowledged for work well-done while fervently protecting their privacy. |
| 10. **Service-oriented**–A desire to quietly be of service to others in the world. |

held high. She walks the walk and talks the talk, Metal that is. Angelina appears Zen-like, almost cosmic, in both her work and life. Nicely done, Angelina, and here is your Zen bow, respectfully presented, of course.

- **Meryl Streep**–She is revered throughout the world as one of the greatest actors of all time. Metals don't necessarily need to be rewarded for their success, but they do desire people's respect. Although she has been nominated 17 times for the Academy Awards, having her colleagues' respect seems to be enough for her. Her acceptance speeches are sincere with gratitude. No showboating needed for Metal! She maintains a very private life, staying out of the public eye, receiving any accolades from her adoring fans from afar.

  Metals are among some of the best actors in history. They have an ability to transform themselves into many different types of characters. From role to role, Meryl transforms herself with such insight and authenticity that we believe her every time! Respect for Metals is earned, and Meryl has earned hers through her hard work and dedication.

- **Johnny Depp**–He just oozes his Metal coolness on and off the screen. He lives a rock-and-roll lifestyle, and fans love him for it! Whether it is his tattoos, his clothes, or the soft way he speaks, he is Metal all the way. Johnny looks withdrawn on the outside, and he might seem soft on the inside to some, but don't be fooled.

Metals can be hardened on the inside, which we often don't see because they mostly seem to hold back in conversations. Johnny's likely to be as tough as nails when push comes to shove. Water and Fire also appear to belong in his top three elements. The Water gives him a slightly awkward style of movement (walking and gestures) that helped him form one of his most well-loved roles as Captain Jack in *Pirates of the Caribbean*. He reports that his character was fashioned after Keith Richards of the Rolling Stones (who, you guessed it, is Water). His alluring Metal-ness helps him in his more sexy roles, such as in *Chocolat*.

More Metal people who are just so . . . cool

James Dean, Marilyn Monroe, Humphrey Bogart, Nicole Kidman, Dame Maggie Smith, Dame Helen Mirren, Queen Elizabeth II, Peter Jackson, Jane Lynch, singer Amanda Palmer, and comedians Paula Poundstone and Jim Gaffigan.

These Metals are the superstars of the celebrity world.

## Water—Stand up or sit down

Water loves drama. Drama, drama, and comedy—or, as we like to call it, dramedy! It's no wonder they top the lists of the world's most celebrated people and entertainers. Waters love to do intense things, whether performing in comedy, movies, theater, or sports. They're visible in every walk of life that involves any kind of dramatic performance from center stage to the big sports arenas worldwide. Privately, they can be very different energetically speaking, exhibiting a more awkward or quirky side than the public persona they portray. Many Waters would prefer to rehearse their scripts rather than talk extemporaneously and clumsily. Hand them a script, something rather exciting and fun, and they will produce a stellar performance without a hitch. Whether it's slapstick or stand-up, Waters rule in the comedy realm. They just love to make people laugh.

### How to Spot a Water

When looking for Water celebrities, notice how they skate across the ground, with all their power in their low backs pushing their hips forward. You can also observe the characteristics listed in the table on the following page.

## 10 Qualities to Watch in Water

| Look for... |
|---|
| 1. **Awkwardness**–Stopping and hesitating speech interspersed with intense surges of speedy phrases. |
| 2. **Nervousness**–Laughing nervously in conversations. Loves to laugh (sometimes hysterically with someone else). |
| 3. **Trend-setting**–Wearing cutting edge and sometimes quirky fashion. Doing and thinking things others don't dare to, yet! |
| 4. **Slapstick**–Not being afraid to be really silly, even in public. |
| 5. **Relentlessness**–Possessing the intense focus and concentration needed to develop skills. |
| 6. **Ambitious**–Desiring to do many things yet might not get off the couch to implement specific goals. |
| 7. **Blunt**–Looking deceivingly shy but might burst out boldly with courageous comments or thoughts. |
| 8. **Adventurous**–Often enjoying intense experiences. |
| 9. **Present**–Living in the now moment. Difficult to draw them out to talk about uncomfortable memories from the past. |
| 10. **Prepared**–Knowing instinctively what to do in emergencies. |

This was a hard list to pick from, but here are a few stellar Waters to laugh with . . .

- *Justin Timberlake*–This Water boy is sexy and smart. His love of adventure and mixing things up in his life is a great example of Water's love of intensity. In addition to his careers as a music superstar and film actor, Justin is drawn to comedy and humor as a regular guest host on Saturday Night Live, even making the elusive Fivers Club in SNL history.

Water is often the first to start new fashions, and Justin is a good example. He launched his own clothing label (William Rast) in 2005 with a friend, giving him a true runway for showing off his forward-looking design concepts. Let's just say, he's the Justin of all trades. There's nothing he won't do if he wants to do it. Water is about having fun, and JT's true and authentic way of living his Water Element shows us all just how much fun one person can have in life!

- **Tiger Woods**—Tiger is a great example of an athletic Water person. Waters are very impressionable, usually going with the flow of those around them, so, often successful Water people will have strong parents backing them. Tiger started sports at a very young age with the strong guidance of his father (a Wood person) in sports and the gentle influence of his mother in spirituality—raising Tiger in the Buddhist religion. Tiger has used his Water strengths to the max to achieve his amazing athletic career that is still soaring today.

Golf, his sport of choice, is perfect for a Water person. During the golf season, he regularly entertains millions, showing them how Waters love periods of intensity followed by moments of rest, over and over again. (If you think golf is boring, watch Tiger play on a Sunday afternoon in front of screaming crowds.) Water is the Element of skill and ability, qualities that shine brightly in Tiger's athletic endeavors. His skills and focus are amazing in golf, and he is reported to love many different sports, including tennis and basketball, which he plays regularly with famous athlete friends throughout the world. On his Watery path, he is already a legendary superstar!

- **Whoopi Goldberg**—Whoopi really shows how Water is always stopping and starting, always flowing, always moving. In many of her movies and performances, her characters are awkward in conversation, holding back, and then talking speedily without stopping. She has the classic monotone Water voice that mostly groans on until interrupted with bursts of intensity.

    When performing her comedy shows, her calm, cool exterior is pervasive, demonstrating that she's in control of others and herself as she changes from her lineup of different characters and personas effortlessly. Whoopi's perfect comedic timing and acting talents continue to entertain millions of people every day with her distinctive "view" on life. She shows us that "it's all good."

More quirky-cool Water people you just gotta love . . . (or not!)

Jack Black, Jay-Z, Jennifer Lawrence, Russell Brand, Miley Cyrus, Jim Carey, Zooey Deschanel, Demi Moore, Robin Williams, Björk, Quentin Tarantino, Kevin Hart, George Bush (Jr. and Sr.), Ronald Reagan, and Angela Merkel (Chancellor of Germany).

These are all powerful and amazing people with their ambitious, talented, and funny Water energy taking the world by storm.

## Stack me up

All these celebrities we mention are more than just their primary Elements. They are multi-faceted, and utilize the strengths of all their Elements, especially their top three Elements in their Elemental stack. For example, let's take a closer look at Oprah Winfrey, Beyoncé, and Justin Timberlake. Let's see how they, well, stack up!

- **Oprah Winfrey**—Wood, Earth, Fire. This Wood Motivator uses her second and third Elements (Earth and Fire) to her advantage on many levels. Her Earth Element was always apparent in the insightful, thought-provoking questions she asked on her daily show. Oprah is also socially astute, knowing, seemingly instinctively, exactly what is appropriate to say in a given moment, sometimes even putting people in their place when they're acting unsuitably or transgressing her sense of moral values.

  Oprah's Fire energy shines in how she creates an almost instant and true connection with the people she interviews. She gently leads them through the interview, making them feel at ease with her light humor, connecting in her caring and trusting way. She has the boldness and quick wit of Wood, the sociability and philosophical thinking of Earth, plus the emotional intelligence and lightness of Fire. Strong, sociable, and connected—that's how Oprah stacks up Elementally speaking.

- **Beyoncé**—Earth, Wood, Water. Beyoncé is more than a sweet, sociable, community-building Earth woman who can sing. She's a strong, powerful performer who continually draws upon her Wood strength and Water energy. Whenever a person has Wood and Water in their top three Elements, watch out! They are an energetic force to be reckoned with. Just observe Beyoncé walk across the stage. Sure, her hips might be moving side to side, but she marches quickly like she's going somewhere and will seemingly run you down if you get in the way.

From our observations, Beyoncé has Earth, Water and Wood in her top three Elements, making her one of the most influential movers and shakers (pun intended) to watch in the world today.

- **Justin Timberlake**—Water, Fire, Earth. Justin's living a fun, adventure-filled, and totally unpredictable Water life. As with anyone else, his First Element isn't all he is. He's also a highly social person, which shows that he puts his Fire and Earth energies (second and third Elements) to work as well. His sociability is often apparent when he's conversing with people. Even when he walks into a room, his smile is so infectious that his adoring fans seems to fall in love with him wherever he goes.

  He's not as quiet as some Waters can be, since his Fire makes him very talkative. His Earth contributes to his ability to work with teams of people. Behind the fun and silliness of his comedic side is a part that is more thoughtful (Earth), and he often engages in deeper and more meaningful conversations.

## Cousin Joey is just like Brad Pitt?

When writing *Connecting Your Circle* and our other book, *The Energy of Love* (Llewellyn, May 2014), we spent countless hours watching and studying celebrities and famous people on TV, in movies, and in on-line interviews to determine their Elemental Energy types. As you develop your own skills, you can apply them to your circle of family, friends, and co-workers.

With practice, the process gets easier and easier. When you are trying to figure out your Cousin Joey's primary Element, you might have to admit that he doesn't look much like Brad Pitt, but he might surprise you in ways, walking and moving a lot like Brad, energetically speaking, that is. This would more than likely put the Wood Element among Cousin Joey's top two Elements.

Just a side note for those interested in doing some on-line homework: If you want to look up some of the celebrities referenced in this chapter, we highly recommend watching interviews with talk-show hosts or observing celeb behavior at events instead of relying on their performances on stage, in the movies, or on TV. Remember, you are watching professional actors and musicians who wear public masks and have public personas. They may appear quite different from who they really are in their private lives. If you want to know their true energies, find them when they're talking in more relaxed settings. We find that watching them walk and listening to them talk when they don't have a predetermined script is usually the best way to evaluate their true Elements. So, put on your celeb-watcher cap. Start with your favorites. We think you will be surprised to learn just how closely you match your favorite, Elementally speaking, of course.

Connecting Your *Circle*

# CONNECTING
# *YOUR* CIRCLE

In an ideal world we would all be able to live, play, and just *be* all of our Five Elements. We would all burst forth in Spring, mature in Summer, relax in the Fall, hibernate in Winter, and transition easily between all these energetic phases.

While this is an admirable goal to work towards, we don't naturally exhibit all Five Elemental energies. Our energy manifests a primary Elemental energy more strongly than all the others throughout our lives. Accepting who you are Elementally is part of your journey to living a more authentic life. It is one part of your life you can enhance but in our view cannot change. It is who you truly are in this lifetime. If you are Wood, you have a natural affinity for Spring and your growth is continual. If you're Fire, you are maturity. You exemplify Summer and all its beauty. If you are Earth, you are the late Summer harvest and the essence of nature's bounty. If you are Metal, you are Autumn. You are the letting go and the nostalgic connection. If you are Water, you are Winter and intensity. You are constantly juxtaposing motion with stillness.

We believe the world needs you to play a part . . . your Elemental energetic part. You have a purpose, a role to play in the bigger picture of the world around you! Can you imagine a world without the Wood Element? How would anything get started? Who would hold the vision of where a project is going? Who would make the to-do lists and delegate? How about a world without Fire? It's like a world without parties, beauty, and fun! Earth is the rock-solid problem solver that everyone counts on. Metal is the knight errant who will come to save the day. And finally, Water is the unpredictable *tour de force* that moves everyone along. Whatever your primary Element is, the rest of the world needs you, and you need all the other Elements to play their parts too, so we all can thrive and grow together in perfect synergy. Okay, maybe we're being a little melodramatic or idealistic here . . . but if you think about the possibility—it is how the world works.

Have you ever noticed that not everyone wants to do the same careers in life? That is a good thing! If we all wanted to do the same jobs, how would the world function? When we do what we enjoy and what we are naturally good at, we play a part that is needed by the whole system to function. We are all energetically different in so many ways, yet we come together each playing our different energetic roles as we cycle through the seasons, year after year since the beginning of time. Think of the cycle as the ongoing Elemental circle of life.

The first and most important reason to learn the Five Elements is to understand who you are energetically and embrace the role you naturally fit into in life. Once you learn to do that more consciously, you can choose to learn about your other Elements, and how to use them to your benefit in your life.

Here's an example of how you can use the tools and knowledge of *Connecting Your Circle.* Imagine working with someone who pushes your buttons, rubs you the wrong way, or just plain ruins your day on a regular basis. They might not have even offended or harmed you in any specific way, it's just something about them. You feel an animosity towards them simply due to their presence in the same room with you. Now let's say that the person is Wood (not to pick on Wood because you might have an aversion to any Elemental Energy type). This Wood pushes ahead in the world, seemingly taking whatever they want, while you wait patiently for your turn. Maybe this Wood gets promoted first when it was clearly your turn. You might find yourself grumbling, "The nerve of them. They just do whatever the heck they like!" You are furious. You are reacting to their actions simply because you don't relate to what is normal behavior for someone with their Elemental Energy type.

How does this anger affect your working relationship? Your relationship might suffer—your work might suffer. Your whole life is being affected. Unless you learn to change or shift your energies to better accommodate this Wood's communication style, things are not going to get better. With your newly acquired knowledge of the Five Elements, you may be able to turn this difficult situation into a smooth and productive one—something more positive. Previously, you have just reacted to this Wood person's energy with thinly veiled animosity or even with out-of-control anger.

Now, by understanding your own Elemental energy and that of Wood, and all that it entails, you work to garner a win-win situation for everyone. Your interpersonal communications are at a whole new level. With your knowledge of the Five Elements, you can stay in control of the situation. You can puff out your chest, walk up to this Wood person, and give them a firm but friendly handshake. Wood almost always will respond well to such gestures energetically, and then you can conduct your business with a win-win attitude. In other words, you put aside your knee-jerk reactions and rise above a bad situation. Everything can be easier for both of you. It will take some work on your part, but when you know more about the Five Elements and how they affect you and all around you, the world suddenly is an easier place to live in.

When you expand yourself and learn to use and master your other four energies, you can connect *your* energetic circle. In any given moment, you will be able to draw upon the energy of any of the Five Elements. Life can be less reactive and less stressful when you flow easily and effortlessly using the Five Elements. Here are some examples of how to employ the full range of Five Element energies to your benefit in common life situations.

## Using your Wood Element

Let's say you are a very chill Metal person, and it's time to buy that new car. You dread having to even speak to anyone at the car dealership, never mind the flock of salespeople you know are waiting to accost you at the door. You have put this task off long enough. You need a new car. You need to zone into your Wood energy to negotiate and have that I-am-not-giving-up-until-I-get-the-best-deal-ever attitude. With your Wood energy at work, you know they will bend. Granted it might take four hours and meeting the entire sales staff with several hushed conversations behind closed doors, but you will have the cleverness, wit, and stamina to conquer! You will drive home in that new car with the knowledge that you did the best you could and got an amazing deal, thanks to your Wood energy! This doesn't mean you always have to be so assertive. You can hang back, be your true Metal self just watching the world while driving around in your new car!

## Using your Fire Element

What if you are Metal, and you need to give a big speech at your company's annual event. Uh-oh! Public speaking sends shivers down your spine? Well, just put on your funny and attractive Fire storytelling hat. Put your heart into your speech and really try to make people care about what you are saying, no matter what the subject matter is. You will be the darling of the evening! No worries if the speech is not perfect! If you channel your Fire, you will certainly *look* fabulous and smile all night long!

## Using your Earth Element

All right, let's say the holidays are fast approaching and your family is in a tizzy. You are Wood, and you really don't want emotional holiday drama. You can draw upon your Earth energies to summon a much-needed family meeting and use your problem-solving, consensus-building (make everyone listen without yelling at them) communication skills to create one big happy family again. Solving problems, including family problems, is something Earths excel at. So, give yourself a nice pat on the back after your family is in the holiday spirit again.

## Using your Metal Element

What if you are Fire and have to go to traffic court for that unfair erroneous speeding ticket. Your smiling face didn't get you out of that jam this time. (What was that cop thinking anyway?) Well, sharpen your Metal energies for this encounter and make the judge want to respect you. You know you're a good citizen, but your posture and the way you present yourself with quiet Metal composure will be a big help. Explaining in the most respectful of ways what really happened, paying attention to details and the rules, will give you the best chances to get the results you want. Many judges are themselves Metal, so you are already ahead of the game!

### Using your Water Element

Let's say you are Earth, someone who likes to solve problems through thoughtful analysis and intelligent, but slow, planning. What if you're suddenly thrown into an emergency situation? You need to make split-second decisions based on what you instinctively know you should do. This is the gift of the Water Elemental Energy type. Waters instinctively know exactly what to do in most emergencies. You just believe that you are doing the right thing, that you will instinctively make the right choice, and you will find yourself in a much better place, energetically. As an Earth person, you can learn to develop these aspects in yourself, even if your natural tendencies are quite the opposite.

## Exercises for Connecting Your Circle

Here are some exercises to help you work on your journey of *Connecting Your Circle*. These exercises are a good place to start to sharpen the range of your Elemental skills. However, we do recommend you read the other books in this series. They will help guide you to become more proficient in identifying the Elements in yourself and in others.

## The journey to the center of you

If you want to *really* feel how the energy of each Element works, you need to recognize the actual strengths and sensations of each of the Elemental energies in your body. While you naturally gravitate toward your primary Element type, you have the ability to move according to each of the other Five Elemental energies. Some Elements are easier than others (your Second Element is probably the easiest to switch into while your Fifth Element will likely be difficult). With these short exercises, you can practice holding your energy in the five different Elemental centers of your body. When you do this, you'll actually feel different, more like that Element! Try it . . .

- **Wood**–Focus your energy in your diaphragm just below your chest and above your stomach. Puff out that area until you feel your elbows move away from your body. When you center your energy in your diaphragm, you feel a surge of confidence. You just can't help but feel stronger and ready to take on the challenge!

- **Fire**—Pull your energy up, up, up into your shoulders like tiny champagne bubbles rising from a newly uncorked bottle. Lift your eyebrows and smile. You can't help but feel joy when you do! Warning: you may start giggling for no apparent reason. Life is good, be happy.

- **Earth**—Plant your feet firmly on the ground and imagine you're connected energetically deep down in the Earth. Now pull all your energy into the center of your belly. Center yourself for a second or two, and then relax, allowing your stomach to stick out like you have a Buddha belly! Feel the warmth and softness, gathering your energy there. You can't help but feel connected and held close to the energy and knowledge of mother Earth herself. Enjoy this feeling, knowing you are going to enjoy helping others. Go ahead, rub that round Buddha belly. It feels good.

- **Metal**—Roll your shoulders back so your chest expands. Lift your chin and then lift your head toward the heavens, eyes looking forward. Imagine you're suspended from a string connecting the top of your head to the clouds above you. Totally relax your arms, let them dangle down, flopping at your sides. Walk like you're floating on a big puffy cloud, letting your body relax. You can't help but feel mellow and reverent. Respect comes to those who earn it.

- **Water**–Push all your energy into your low back, your kidneys. We want you to feel that energy building and revving up like a powerful engine ready to propel you at a moment's notice. Revving but not moving, ready, ready, ready . . . vroom, vroom. You can't help but feel a surge of power that makes you feel awake and aware, anticipating what's next. Be prepared to feel a little anxious about all the things you can do in this hyper state of awareness. For the slower energy Water types, just go lie down on the couch and think about all the things you will get done when you're finished napping. Chill.

## Mission: Not impossible

Here is your mission . . . another fun way to study the other Elements is to become an apprentice to five of your friends, each one representing a different Elemental Energy type. We are not talking about the TV show with Donald Trump (who is über Wood) called *The Apprentice* but more about having quality hanging out time with your circle of family or friends–Elemental style. We invite you to become a master observer, a quiet detective uncovering facts, a fly on the wall, so to speak. You will be their student in the crash course of what their life is like on a day-to-day basis.

If you choose to accept this fun, little *mission*, here are some general tips for success. Try to observe without judgment, without comments, without complaining along the way. Receiving permission to glimpse someone's private life is a privilege. Make it your mission to observe everything about your subjects. How do they walk? How do they talk? What do they like to do in their spare time? What kind of music do they listen to? What kind of people do they have around them? What is their favorite kind of ice cream? Yes, you should eat that flavor too (just this once if you can). What does the inside of their house look like? What does the inside of their car look like? What kinds of things do they keep in their cabinets? How do they decorate? What do they like to do for fun? Listen, really listen, to what they like to talk about. If they don't like to talk much and enjoy getting out and doing things, then experience life with them the way they do it . . . emulating their actions and reactions. Try to do it with the same energy level they bring to life—matching and moving with them. Pay attention to how each Element is different, including your own Element. The following is a discussion of what to look for in each Element to help you make this mission totally possible.

- For your **Wood** Element friend, you will need to behave with the same high energy and purpose they put into their activities—a sporting event, participating in a race (of any kind), or even playing an intense game of ping-pong. If you don't like to compete normally, you can try to develop your Wood strengths by participating in competitions with them or on your own. The point of competing isn't to beat someone else but to find a way everyone can win. Set a goal that's a bit of a stretch but still safe and achievable.

  Get in touch with your own confidence and be assertive so you can make things happen. Embrace and hang onto a continual state of hope, pushing you to action with a can-do attitude. Woods can have a lot of energy, and sometimes put in long days filled with many different activities. Pay attention to how Woods set goals for themselves. Take these goals as seriously as they do and really push yourself (again, in a safe way). The Wood mantra could easily be, "Just do it," and so should you if you want to understand Wood just a little better.

- Join your **Fire** Element friends when they're doing something social and exciting. It could be a day out shopping for new clothes or going to a comedy club and not caring how loud you laugh in public! Can you laugh with as much sincerity and genuine enthusiasm as they do? Can you muster the same level of excitement and passion they have? We've all had the experience of faking excitement around someone who's more excited than you are. But can you really *feel* as excited as they are? If so, then you've found your Fire Element!

  Fire is about joy, excitement, or contented happiness. Imagine you have a bright light emanating from inside. Your eyes are bright, you're smiling, and you want to share laughter with everyone you meet. To hang out with most Fires, you have to love social events and having fun in large groups of people. Occasionally Fires will be in a more inward phase in their lives, when they are smoldering like coals and not blazing like a bonfire. Fire has a full range of liveliness, but the point of developing your Fire is to go into a festive mode. Imagine people looking at you and how you want to appear. Then dress up. Wear red (even if you're a guy)! Take the time to do your hair and dress as attractively as possible. When you arrive at your event, watch all the people. Focus on them. The Bobby McFerrin song, *Don't Worry, Be Happy*, could be one of the theme songs for Fires.

- Join your **Earth** friends at a local community event or attend a lecture with them where you will learn something. The best events occur when everyone sits in a circle-like setting, taking turns talking, sharing, drumming, or singing. You get the idea. If you dislike group dynamics, push yourself into a group of Earth people anyway. Adopt the role of someone who really cares about everyone else getting their turn. Listen attentively to what people are saying. Then prepare to go on problem-solving adventures with them. They love to make things better in the world. They are the fixers.

  To play your role, you'll need patience; you'll need to chill out. Share the air space with everyone, and learn to take your time, indulging yourself in being unhurried. Allow yourself to just go with the flow, looking at everything through their eyes, noticing what they find important to take into account in their problem-solving process. To use another example, if your Earth friend decides to go, say, on a shopping fest, be prepared to spend over an hour in a single small store! Relax, there's no rush. Spend time observing your Earth friends in many other settings as well. Look at how they use their knowledge to evaluate a situation and make things better.

Use your mind and your ears to listen. Earth people are attentive listeners so they can understand others. They like being helpful and having something to give that people need and appreciate. But they are more than a bundle of feelings and emotions. They also use their brains, trying to wrap their heads around problems before settling on a solution. Listen to them, and process things alongside of them. Make yourself a partner in their problem-solving efforts, talking over the issues, strategies, and solutions, all the while using a reflective part of your mind to learn from them. "Caring is sharing" is a happy motto of many Earthies.

- **Metal** friends might want to take you on a road trip to visit a sacred place, like a temple, an old barn, a museum, or even a graveyard. (Visiting a graveyard with a Metal person can be an amazing experience!) Observe how they quietly move into a space. Their silence speaks volumes. Try to share in the moment as they do, saying few words, as if you had joined them in a vow and bond of silence. Breathe, and just be. Observe and relax.

    Listen to what your Metal friends are listening to musically. Touch what they are touching. Eat what they are eating. Watch how they like to follow all the rules of the places they visit. Be prepared to be a goody-two-shoes. (For Metals, sneaking into the museum without paying full price is a big no-no.) See what they see and experience as they do. Try to be Zen-like, internalizing the exquisite and sublime beauty they find in the world. They inhabit a state of cosmic connection. With them as your teacher, learn to appreciate the valuable and awe-inspiring. You will be cool without even trying. That is the Metal mystique.

- When it's time to hang with your **Water** friends, you are probably, maybe unwittingly, entering the start gate of a fun and exciting adventure . . . or not. Be prepared for anything from rock climbing at the local gym to white-water rafting, to maybe a video game marathon on the couch. Go along with them in the flow of the moment. It might push your boundaries to do something that scares you–but don't worry . . . you can trust in Water. They are the safety monitors of the Elemental world.

Let go, try it, and see the world from their eyes of anticipation. It's usually exciting to feel that something extraordinary is about to happen but don't expect Water types to take you on a perpetual roller-coaster ride. Instead you'll likely alternate between intense activity and lying around resting as you recover from your latest adventure. But when the peak moments of experience return, remember to act as an observer while absorbing what's happening. Watch how your Water friends are so alive in that moment. Be that alive with them. Then be chill and get ready to talk about the next adventure! "It's all good" and "wait 'til next time" could be the feelings you get, and that truly is a good thing!

## Music to your ears

Your next exercise is one of our favorite Elemental activities. Music is vibrational and has qualities similar to energy. Music often reflects one of the Elemental signatures. Some music is consistently one Element (usually songs sung by one person), or some songs combine a variety of Elemental energies, reflecting the energetic types of all the band members playing them. But music itself exhibits energy movement through sound and vibrations as it comes to life.

Listening to music on the way to work? How about enjoying your morning (or afternoon) drive while furthering your Five Element studies? To identify the Elemental quality of a song, ask yourself some questions while listening. What energy does the song have?

- Does it have a forceful, marching beat, like the **Wood** Element? Wood songs tend to have heavy down beats and a strong energy to them. Famous Wood singers include: Lady Gaga, Pink, Madonna, Eminem, Frank Sinatra, and Jennifer Lopez.

- Does the song feel upbeat and bouncy? **Fire** music tends to be about Fire's favorite topic: Love! (Or, even more popular . . . lost love!) Many modern pop songs have this boppy, light feeling that is the Fire Element. Famous Fires in music include:

Elton John, Paul McCartney, Janis Joplin, Freddy Mercury, Barbara Streisand, Bette Midler, Justin Bieber, Robert Plant, and Usher.

- Soft and rhythmical is **Earth's** kind of music. The songs often have repetitive beats, like Latin or African music. They make you want to move your hips circularly, like in Salsa dancing. Well known Earth musicians include: Beyoncé, Bono (of U2), Bruce Springsteen, Norah Jones, Christina Aguilera, Shakira, and Michael Franti.

- **Metal's** type of music can have funky beats. Other Metal music, like Blues music, is in the minor key, making you nostalgic. The songs range from intense and angry heavy metal to ballads of loss and remembrance to mellow jazz. Famous Metal singers are often the coolest out there, including: John Lennon, Neil Young, Leonard Cohen, Joni Mitchell, Hope Sandoval of Mazzy Star, Amanda Palmer, MIA, and Beth Orton.

- When you hear a lot of complexity in the music with varied instruments and beats overlaying each other, think **Water**. Water music will often start slow and build to an intense crescendo.

The music is powerful but playful, and sometimes even silly. Genres that tend to be more Water-like are intense jazz, classical, new age, some punk, and very fast-talking rap. Famous Water musicians include: Justin Timberlake, Bob Marley, Miley Cyrus, Jay-Z, Cyndi Lauper, Yo-Yo Ma, Björk, and The Pixies.

## Seeing the world with new eyes

For hundreds of years, the ancient Chinese masters observed the energy and movement of life. Their legacy of over two thousand years, is the theory of the Five Elements, which gives us an effective set of tools for understanding and accepting ourselves. Remember those three little words, "Who are you?" that we asked you at the beginning of this book? We hope this series of books will get you much closer to answering that question authentically and lovingly. We truly want to see you living more in your own Element than ever before.

Once you understand your Elemental energy, you don't have to stop there. The Chinese also believed that you could become a Sage (like a wizard or very wise person) by mastering your energy through understanding and developing all the Five Elements in yourself, which we call *Connecting Your Circle*.

These Chinese sages were revered throughout Chinese history for their wisdom.

You too can master the Five Elements. Once you open your eyes to the Elemental energies circulating and moving all around you, you can begin to use your new skills to make every communication and interaction easier and more comfortable. You can adapt yourself energetically to another person yet *still be* authentic and true to yourself. People who connect their circle are not misrepresenting themselves when they draw upon their less dominant elemental traits to address a particular situation, for all the Elements are part of who they truly are. Sometimes people will disagree, but in general, disagreements can be resolved if people can attune to each other's Elemental styles in a way that sustains rather than subverts relationships. Yes, you may get your way because you're not energetically butting heads with the other person anymore, and you are working *with* rather than *against* that person's energy. Forcing or bullying your way through life's interactions is not what we are talking about but rather a gentle flow of life that can be assertive yet fair.

We recommend you read our book, *The Energy of Love* (Llewellyn, 2014), which explains the ways the Five Element energies interact at a much deeper level in interpersonal communications. Some energies are compatible and nourishing to each other. Others are controlling, often causing misunderstanding or contention. When you have achieved mastery over the Five Elemental energies within you, you will have the ability to avert negative dynamics and support win-win collaborations with others.

Harnessing and mastering the power of all Five Elements is truly possible. It's not just a novelty—something to learn about and forget—but something to have fun with, live with, and be immersed in everyday. It is who you are in life, giving you new perspective on the world. And who knows? If you continue learning the Five Elements in yourself, you may eventually become that Sage, someone who is a true master of their life. Think of Yoda from Star Wars, who says, "May the Force be with you"... only now you are the *force*! The *qi* runs through you. It all comes down to understanding the way energy works in the real world. And last time we checked, it *appears* we're all still in the real world. Well, most of us anyway.

# In Appreciation

We are deeply grateful to all who helped make this book come to life. Our heart-felt thanks go to Dr. Steve Herman and Jennifer Abbingsole, our tireless copyeditors who always said, "Bring it on," and, "Who needs sleep anyway?" Our thanks also go to the tireless sleeping (and snoring) at our feet provided by Ace, our number one doggie fan. Special muchas gracias to our smiling friends Adie and Erick at Nautilus and Baggi and Nico at Otro Lado in Santa Teresa for their amazing hospitality in the final days before publishing this book. We felt like we'd landed in nirvana.

## Leta

I am eternally grateful to Jaye for bringing her brilliant writing talent to this project. Her ability to be 100 percent engaged in everything made this book's creation fun and easy! She mastered the Five Elements faster and more thoroughly than anyone I've ever known, and her partnership in delivering this work has opened up my eyes to new ways the Five Elements can help all of us.

To my amazing teacher Jeffrey Yuen, who taught me with a wonderful sense of humor and clarity to open my mind as well as my heart to limitless possibilities. His wisdom was both healing and transformative at a key transition time in my life. Thanks also to my clients—my life teachers. Our one-on-one soul searching has brought so many "Aha" moments to understanding the Five Elements and the workings of each individual soul's search for authenticity.

Thanks to the many before me who dedicated their lives to the Five Elements: to J.R. Worsley, who brought the Five Element wisdom to the West; to Elizabeth Rochat de la Vallée and Claude Larre, whose improved translations of the ancient texts were instrumental to my understanding of the Five Elements; to Eliot Cowan, for introducing me to the Five Elements many years ago, and finally to Niki

Bilton, who assimilated the teachings of many and took my understanding of the Five Elements to a whole new level.

To Dunan Herman-Parks for teaching me, "It's all good, Mom" every day of his beautiful life. Thanks to my parents, Gail and Steve Herman, for their unconditional Fire love. I've been so fortunate to know that I'm loved every day of my life. To Neal Parks for his dedication to everything I've become. To Sandra Hoover for her love and support over these many years.

To my friends Jill Goldreyer for pointing me on the healing path, and Sally Hopkins Connor for being there for me from the start, my *tour de force*. Thanks to all my friends all over the world for all the love, laughter, and positive energy you send every day. Thank you.

## Jaye

Leta, Cara, Dax (and Ace) . . . The spark, the rock, and the barks.

Leta for asking me to share in this amazing project and making me laugh every day. Your light is so bright, the whole world can see it shining! Your brain works like no one I have ever met; you are inspiring! Thank you for helping me find my inner Yoda.

Cara Niederberger for being the most understanding, positive, loving person I will ever meet. Thank you, thank you, thank you.

# About the Authors

LETA HERMAN is an author, Five Elements and Chinese Medicine teacher, nationally certified acupressure practitioner, and co-author of *The Energy of Love* (Llewellyn 2014). She has immersed herself in the philosophies of Daoism, Alchemical Healing, and Chinese Medicine, as well as many other healing modalities. A Smith College graduate and past nationally syndicated journalist, Herman has devoted the past fifteen years to learning everything possible about the Five Elements. In other aspects of life, Leta is also a world explorer who speaks multiple languages, loves life, her family, and a challenging game of Boggle.

JAYE McELROY is an author, photographer, business entrepreneur and co-author of *The Energy of Love* (Llewellyn 2014). She has completely integrated the Five Elements into her unique practice as a Five Element Life Coach. McElroy combines her career in advertising, business, and writing with the Five Elements to help people manifest their true potential in life. She considers herself a humble student of life, love, her dog Dax and of course the Five Elements. It has recently been discovered that one of her secret wishes in life is to travel through time and space in the Tardis with the Doctor.

www.ConnectingYourCircle.com

For more information on the soon to be released 2014 Five Element Series "*So You think you are...*" by Leta & Jaye please visit:

www.ConnectingYourCircle.com

**Also by
Leta Herman & Jaye McElroy**

LETA HERMAN & JAYE McELROY

the energy of

Love

APPLYING THE FIVE ELEMENTS
TO TURN ATTRACTION INTO
TRUE CONNECTION

Want it, find it, keep it

Available in
bookstores & online.

www.TheEnergyofLoveBook.com

Printed in Great Britain
by Amazon

48462204R00075